Southern Lotus
VERY DEMURE
VERY SPOOKY

Share your masterpieces with us.
Join our group "Southern Lotus Coloring Community"
on Facebook group.

Scan the QR code
for more information

 @southernlotus.publishing   Southern Lotus Coloring Book

1000+ FREE DIGITAL COLORING PAGES!

Grateful for your choice!

Visit the SOUTHERN LOTUS COLORING COMMUNITY Facebook group to download them.

PAPER SELECTION

We select standard-quality paper to keep our products affordable due to the limited options available on Amazon. If you experience bleeding with certain pens or markers, placing a blank sheet of thicker paper behind the page can help.

We are grateful for your understanding of our paper selection!

Coloring takes us to a world where freedom, creativity, and self-expression really pop, giving us a fun break from all the modern-day stress. It has not just become a relaxing activity but a must-have in our daily routine.

TODAY will be a GOOD DAY

 SHARE WITH US!

Your unique style makes every coloring page special. We'd love to see your creations! Drop some pictures with your feedback so we can enjoy the awesome work of a creative artist like you!

SCAN TO JOIN WITH US

Southern Lotus

CONNECT WITH US

Please feel free to reach out to us if you have any questions.

coloring@southernlotus.com

STEPS FOR BETTER COLORING!

Step 1: Pick your favorite page and coloring medium.

Step 2: Place a blank sheet under the page you're coloring to avoid bleeding and imprints on the next page.

Tip: Flip to the last bonus blank page of this book, and tear it out

Step 3: Color your own way!

Thank you for your attention. HaPPY coloring!

THIS BOOK BELONGS TO

....

THIS BOOK BELONGS TO

TEST COLOR PAGE

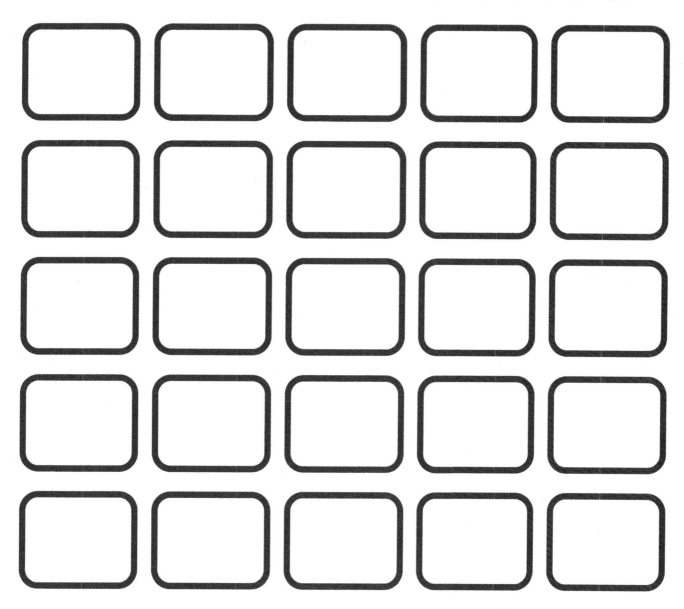

TEST COLOR PAGE

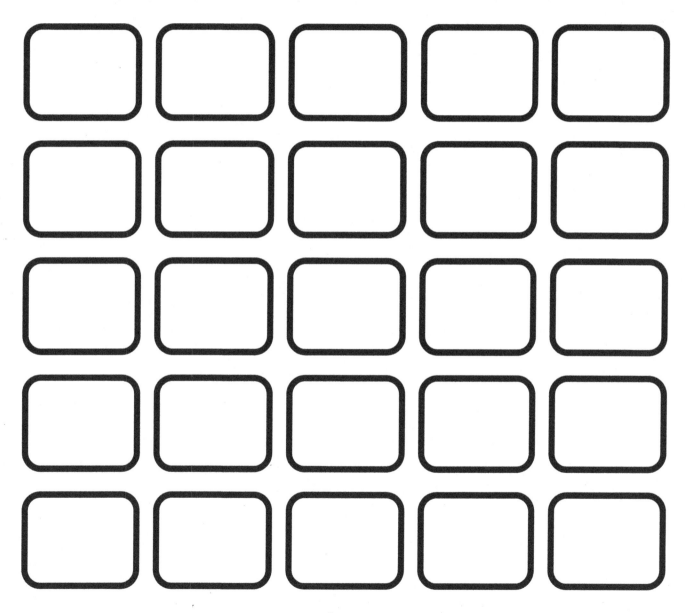

Use this paper underneath to prevent ink seepage and maintain the integrity of your creation (Optional)

BOLD AND EASY COLLECTION

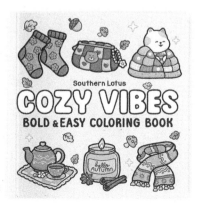

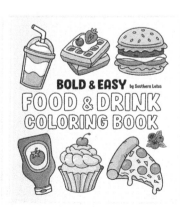

Made in the USA
Monee, IL
06 November 2024